C A P S T O N E   P R E S S
818 North Willow Street • Mankato, Minnesota 56001

Printed in the United States of America.

Library of Congress Cataloging-in-Publication Data
Mara, W. P.
   Chameleons/by William P. Mara.
   p. cm.
   Includes bibliographical references and index.
   Summary: Describes the physical characteristics, habitat, and behavior of the chameleon lizard.
   ISBN 1-56065-399-X
   1. Chameleons--Juvenile literature. [1. Chameleons.] I. Title. II. Series:
Mara, W. P.
QL666.L23M35 1996
597.95--dc20

                                                96-2047
                                                  CIP
                                                   AC

Photo credits
R.D. Bartlett, 6, 10, 19-25, 28-32, 43. W.P. Mara, cover, 4, 12-17, 26, 37, 45, 47. James P. Rowan, 34, 39.

Chameleons

by W. P. Mara

CAPSTONE PRES

MANKATO, MINNESOTA

Table of Contents

Words in **boldface** type in the text are defined
in the Glossary in the back of this book.

Fast Facts About Chameleons

Scientific Name: Chameleons are lizards. They belong to a family called Chameleonidae.

Physical Features: Chameleons have very long tongues. Their bodies can change color. They are flat on both sides. Their bulging eyes move independently of each other. They have Y-shaped feet.

Reproduction: Males become very colorful at the start of the breeding season. Sometimes males will fight for the right to mate with a particular female. Most chameleons lay eggs, but some give birth to living young. Newborn chameleons are tiny.

Daily Habits: Chameleons are active during the day and sleep at night. They live in trees and bushes. They spend most of their time off the ground. They prefer to live alone rather than in small groups. They usually let food come to them rather than searching for it. They often sit in the sun.

Range: Most chameleons live in Africa or Madagascar. A few others are found in southern Europe, India, Sri Lanka, and Asia Minor.

Habitat: Most chameleons prefer areas where there are many leafy trees and bushes. These give them places to hide. They also prefer to stay close to some permanent water source. They can be found in both very humid and very dry areas.

Life Span: No one knows how long chameleons live in the wild. In captivity, they live up to eight years.

Food: Chameleons are **carnivores**. Their diet includes spiders, grasshoppers, crickets, moths, flies, caterpillars, and locusts.

Chapter 1

Modern Dragons

Chameleons have been on the earth for about 150 million years. They have been around since the time of the dinosaurs. Some people call chameleons modern dragons.

Chameleons can change the color of their skin. They can look both forward and backward at the same time. They can catch insects with their tongues. They can hang by their tails. These talents help them survive.

The word chameleon comes from a Greek word, chamaele. It means little lion. When a

Chameleons have been around since the time of the dinosaurs. Some people call them modern dragons.

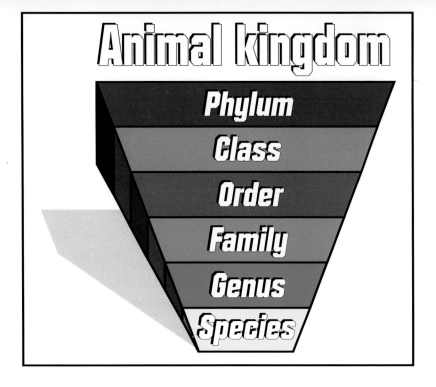

Animal kingdom

- Phylum
- Class
- Order
- Family
- Genus
- Species

chameleon gets very angry, it displays some lionlike qualities. It will hiss and snort. Sometimes it opens up its mouth to show its teeth.

Classification System

Chameleons are lizards. They are a part of the **scientific classification system**. The system can be thought of as an upside-down pyramid. Animals that are most closely related are at the bottom. The largest animal groups are at the top.

At the very top is a huge group known as a **phylum**. Chameleons belong to the Chordata phylum. Just below that is a **class**. Chameleons belong to the Reptile class. Then, there is an **order**. Chameleons belong to an order with snakes and other lizards. The name of the order is Squamata (skwa-MAH-tuh).

After that, there is a **family**. Chameleons belong to the Chameleonidae (kuh-mee-lee-ON-oh-dee) family. Then, there is a **genus**. Finally, at the very bottom, is a **species**. There are nearly 100 different species of chameleons.

All chameleons have Latin names that are also known as scientific names. Some chameleons also have English names that are usually called common names. Some common names are panther chameleon, jewel chameleon, mountain chameleon, and three-horned chameleon.

Chapter 2
Where Chameleons Live

Most chameleons are found in only two places in the entire world. Most live in Africa and on the island of Madagascar. The large island of Madagascar is in the Indian Ocean. It is off the southeast coast of Africa.

There are a few other chameleons in southern Europe, India, Sri Lanka, and Asia Minor. The oldest known **fossil** of a chameleon was found in China. But there are no chameleons in China today.

Chameleons are **Old World** lizards. Think of the earth as being divided in half, from top to bottom. The half that contains Europe, Asia,

This chameleon lives in Madagascar.

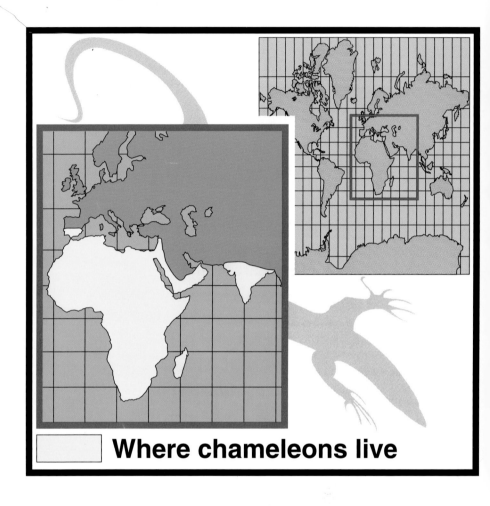

Where chameleons live

Africa, and Australia is the Old World. The half that contains North America and South America is the **New World**.

Introduced Species

One chameleon species, known as Jackson's chameleon, is found in Hawaii. But it did not originate there. A long time ago, someone brought a few chameleons to Hawaii by boat. Then, either accidentally or on purpose, the chameleons got loose. Now, Jackson's chameleon is a normal part of Hawaii's wildlife. It is known as an introduced species, or **alien species**.

Most chameleons live in places where there are many leafy trees and bushes. These give them places to hide. Some live in rain forests. These areas are very hot and humid. Other chameleons live in **savannas** and semidesert regions. These areas are rather dry.

Chapter 3
The Chameleon Body

Chameleons vary in size. The smallest chameleon in the world is barely three-quarters of an inch (two centimeters) long. That is smaller than a full-grown cricket. The largest chameleon species in the world grows to about 2 1/2 feet (76 centimeters) long. That is about as long as the arm of an adult man. Most chameleons are between three and eight inches (8 and 20 centimeters) long.

The body of a chameleon is flat on both sides. A chameleon's back is rounded and often very high. The head on most chameleons is large in comparison to the rest of its body.

Most chameleons have a large head in comparison to the rest of their body.

The eyes of a chameleon bulge out like bubbles. They can move in different directions. This means a chameleon can look behind and in front of itself at the same time.

Toes Help Climb

Chameleons have Y-shaped feet. They have three clawed toes on one side of the Y. They have two clawed toes on the other side of the Y. The toes help a chameleon climb through trees and bushes.

A chameleon's tail can hold onto things when the lizard climbs. When they are not climbing, chameleons keep their tails rolled up in a tight spiral.

A chameleon can wrap its tail around a branch and hang from it. This type of tail is called a **prehensile** tail. Unlike other lizards, a chameleon cannot lose its tail and grow another one. Once a chameleon's tail is gone, it is gone for good.

Chameleons can hang from their prehensile tails.

When a chameleon wants to catch something to eat, it fires out its tongue. The tongue hits the target and sticks to it. Then the chameleon sucks its tongue back in again and swallows its food. The tongue is ball-shaped at the tip. Sometimes the tongue is longer than the chameleon itself.

Changing Colors

Chameleons are usually green, brown, or gray. But they can change color. Some chameleon species can only turn brown or green. Others, however, can turn shades of yellow, orange, white, black, and even blue. They can also add patterns like diamonds and circles.

Chameleons do not change color to hide themselves, as many people once believed. Their normal color helps them stay hidden. Chameleons change colors in response to emotions, light, and temperature.

Some chameleons change into bright colors.

Chameleons change colors when they are angry.

During the breeding season, the males will change colors or patterns to attract a female's attention. Or the male might change colors to frighten off another male when he is competing for a female. Sometimes a female will change colors or patterns when she is not interested in breeding.

Colors Reflect Moods

If a chameleon is afraid or angry, it will change colors or patterns. Different colors can reflect different moods.

Temperatures also affect a chameleon's color. When the weather is cool, chameleons darken their skin. This helps them absorb more heat from the sun. On warm days, chameleons lighten their skin. This helps them reflect the sun's rays.

Male and female chameleons have a few physical differences. The tail of most males is thicker where it connects to the body. Also, many male chameleons have higher-arched backs. They also may have horns on their heads. There are other, smaller differences as well, but they vary from species to species.

Chapter 4

Daily Life

Most chameleons sleep during the night and are active during the day. This means they are diurnal animals. Animals that are active during the night and sleep during the day are called nocturnal animals.

Like most reptiles, chameleons spend a lot of time **basking** in the sun. They do this because they are **cold-blooded**. They need the sun's heat to survive. Their bodies cannot make their own heat. Instead, they have to get their warmth from the sun.

Most chameleons spend almost every minute of their lives in trees and bushes. This is called

Most chameleons live in trees.

an arboreal lifestyle. A female will come down from the trees when she is ready to lay eggs. Also, chameleons will come down to the ground to move to another tree or bush. But they are awkward on the ground. Their feet are made for living in trees.

A few chameleons live on the ground all the time. They have short tails and scales on their feet. They are called stump-tailed chameleons.

Hunting For Food

Chameleons sit quietly when they hunt for food. They wait for their prey to come to them. They blend in with their surroundings. When the prey is close enough, the chameleon's tongue shoots out and catches it.

Most chameleons live on a diet of insects and spiders. They eat grasshoppers, crickets, locusts, caterpillars, moths, dragonflies, and other insects. Large chameleons also eat small birds, mice, and even other lizards.

Chameleons do not have the kind of tongue that lets them lap up water like a dog or a cat. So chameleons do not drink from ponds or

A few chameleons live on the ground all the time.

streams like many other animals. Instead, when they are thirsty, chameleons lick drops of rain or dew from leaves and branches.

Live Alone

Chameleons prefer to live alone. A chameleon will live by itself in a tree or a bush. When another chameleon comes along, the first one will do everything it can to defend its home and its privacy. This is called territorial behavior.

If they need to, chameleons will fight each other.

Chameleons have several ways to scare away enemies. They may change into very bright colors to frighten their attackers. Chameleons can also puff up their bodies and make hissing sounds. If it needs to, a chameleon will scratch and bite its enemy.

Chapter 5
Reproduction

At the start of their breeding season, male chameleons are at their most colorful. His colors are known as breeding colors and are used to attract a female.

Often, a male has to fight with another male to win the right to mate with a certain female. These fights usually do not last long and are not very violent. After a winner has been decided, the loser stalks off. His color often becomes very dark.

Male chameleons are most colorful during the mating season.

Colorful Skin

Bulging Eyes

Y-Shaped Feet

Prehensile Tail

Most Lay Eggs

Once a female has mated with a male, she will either lay eggs or give birth to live young. Most chameleons lay eggs. The chameleons dig holes in the ground. After they lay their eggs in the hole, they cover them with dirt. There can be as many as 50 eggs in one hole. The females then return to their life in the trees. Their job as a parent is over.

After many months the baby chameleons hatch. They climb through the soft dirt to the surface. Then they head for the trees. They are on their own.

Some chameleons give birth to live young. The babies are encased in a thin layer of tissue called a membrane. It looks something like a gum bubble. The mother chameleon sticks the membrane to a tree branch. After several moments, the babies rip the membrane open. They, too, are on their own from the start. Baby chameleons are in great danger during their first year of life. They are often eaten by snakes, birds, or other lizards.

Baby chameleons hatch after spending months in eggs.

Chapter 6

Conservation

Some chameleons are becoming rare. Their natural **habitat** is being destroyed. The trees they live in are being cut down to make room for farms, buildings, and other development. Chameleons are being forced into smaller and smaller areas. Many chameleons are captured and sold as pets. Many die.

There is some hope, however. Laws have been passed that protect wild chameleons. Some countries do not allow people to take chameleons from those countries. Then the chameleons cannot be sold as pets. Laws have

Many chameleons are kept as pets.

been passed to help save chameleons and other animals, too. **Conservation** groups also work to save animals in the wild.

Scientists are trying to breed chameleons in zoos. It is not easy to do. If their efforts are successful, the chameleon will not die out.

Zoo Trips

If you cannot view chameleons in the wild, visit a zoo. A zoo is a great place to learn about lizards and other animals.

Make the most of your zoo trips. Do not just walk around aimlessly. Leave knowing more than you did before your visit.

Take a notebook with you. When you see a lizard that interests you, stand quietly. Watch the lizard. See what it does. Then write down what you see. You can learn a lot about an animal by doing this.

Ask yourself questions. Is the lizard sleeping during the day? If so, it is probably nocturnal. Is the lizard in a cage by itself? Then it probably is a solitary animal and does not usually live in a group. How big is the lizard? What color is it? How does it act? You will be amazed at how much you can learn by observation.

At the zoo, look closely at a chameleon's Y-shaped feet.

If you can, bring a camera with you. A zoo is an excellent place to take pictures of animals. Lizards are beautiful animals. If you are a good artist, sketch pictures during your zoo trip. Photos and drawings of lizards give you visual reminders of your trip. You could put the pictures in a scrapbook and use them later for school projects.

Some of the top zoos in which to view lizards are in Houston, Philadelphia, San Diego, and Washington, D.C. In Canada, two of the top zoos are in Calgary and Toronto. But there are many other wonderful zoos, too. Visit a zoo and enjoy yourself. Trips to the zoo are both fun and educational.

Some of the top zoos in which to view lizards:

Black Hills Reptile Gardens
South Highway 16
Rapid City, SD 57701

Calgary Zoo
1300 Zoo Road NE
P.O. Box 3036 Station B
Calgary, AB T2M 4R8
Canada

Houston Zoological Gardens
1513 Outer Belt Drive
Houston, TX 77030

Metropolitan Toronto Zoo
361A Old Finch Avenue
Scarborough, ON M1B 5K7
Canada

National Zoological Park
3001 Connecticut Avenue NW
Washington, DC 20008

The Philadelphia Zoological Garden
34th Street and Girard Avenue
Philadelphia, PA 19020

The San Diego Zoo
Park Boulevard and Zoo Avenue
Balboa Park
San Diego, CA 92103

Look for the Parson's chameleon at the zoo.

Glossary

alien species—animal or plant that has been brought into an area outside of its natural range and has managed to establish itself there

bask—lie or rest and enjoy a pleasant warmth

carnivore—animal that feeds on the flesh of other animals

class—group of animals or plants that have similar characteristics, ranking above an order and below a phylum

cold-blooded—having a body temperature that changes according to the temperature of the surroundings

conservation—the official care, protection, or management of natural resources

family—group of related plants or animals, ranking above a genus and below an order

fossil—the remains of something that once lived

genus—group of closely related plants or animals, usually including several species

habitat—area in which a plant or animal naturally grows or lives

New World—the Western Hemisphere

Old World—the Eastern Hemisphere

order—group of plants or animals that are similar in many ways, ranking above a family and below a class

phylum—one of the larger groups into which plants and animals are divided, ranking above a class and below a kingdom

prehensile—suitable for grasping or holding, especially by wrapping around something

savanna—flat grassland in warm regions with scattered trees

scientific classification system—the way all living things are listed and categorized

species—group of plants or animals most closely related to each other in the scientific classification system

To Learn More

Barrett, Norman. *Dragons and Lizards.* New York: Franklin Watts, 1991.

Chace, G. Earl. *The World of Lizards.* New York: Dodd, Mead and Co., 1982.

Gravelle, Karen. *Lizards.* New York: Franklin Watts, 1991.

Ivy, Bill. *Lizards.* Our Wildlife World. New York: Grolier, 1990.

Martin, James. *Chameleons: Dragons in the Trees.* New York: Crown Publishers, 1991.

McCarthy, Colin. *Reptile.* An Eyewitness Book. New York: Alfred A. Knopf, 1991.

Schnieper, Claudia. *Chameleons.* Minneapolis: Carolrhoda Books, 1988.

Smith, Trevor. *Amazing Lizards.* New York: Alfred A. Knopf, 1990.

You can read about chameleons in *Reptile Hobbyist* and *Reptile and Amphibian* magazines.

This chameleon lives in Madagascar.

Useful Addresses

African Wildlife Foundation
1717 Massachusetts Avenue NW
Washington, DC 20036

Defenders of Wildlife
1244 Nineteenth Street NW
Washington, DC 20036

The Long Island Herpetological Society
476 North Ontario Avenue
Lindenhurst, NY 11757

Minnesota Herpetological Society
Bell Museum of Natural History
10 Church Street SE
Minneapolis, MN 55455-0104

Ontario Herpetological Society
P.O. Box 244
Port Credit, ON L5G 4L8
Canada

San Diego Herpetological Society
P.O. Box 4036
San Diego, CA 92164-4036

World Nature Association
P.O. Box 673
Silver Spring, MD 20918

This young veiled chameleon fits on a human finger.

Internet Sites

Herp Link
http://home.ptd.net/~herplink/index.html

Maui's Jackson's Chameleon Page
http://www.maui.net/%7Eteam/jackson.html

True Chameleons
http://www.skypoint.com/members/mikefry/
chams2.html

ZooNet
http://www.mindspring.com/~zoonet

Adult veiled chameleons grow very large.

Index